D1706468

Self-Healing Through Visual and Verbal Art Therapy

of related interest

Studio Art Therapy
Cultivating the Artist Identity in the Art Therapist
Catherine Hyland Moon
ISBN 1 85302 814 2

The Artist as Therapist
Arthur Robbins
ISBN 1 85302 907 6

The Changing Shape of Art Therapy
New Developments in Theory and Practice
Edited by Andrea Gilroy and Gerry McNeilly
ISBN 1 85302 939 4

Art-Based Research
Shaun McNiff
ISBN 1 85302 621 2 paperback
ISBN 1 85302 620 4 hardback

The Revealing Image
Analytical Art Psychotherapy in Theory and Practice
Joy Schaverien
ISBN 1 85302 821 5

Healing Arts
The History of Art Therapy
Susan Hogan
Forewords by Mary Douglas and David Lomas
ISBN 1 85302 799 5

Art as Therapy
Collected Papers
Edith Kramer
Foreword by Lani Alaine Gerity
ISBN 1 85302 902 5

Art Therapy with Children on the Autistic Spectrum
Beyond Words
Kathy Evans and Janek Dubowski
ISBN 1 85302 825 8

Self-Healing Through Visual and Verbal Art Therapy

R.M. Simon

Edited by S.A. Graham

Jessica Kingsley Publishers
London and Philadelphia

All rights reserved. No part of this publication may be reproduced in any material form (including photocopying or storing it in any medium by electronic means and whether or not transiently or incidentally to some other use of this publication) without the written permission of the copyright owner except in accordance with the provisions of the Copyright, Designs and Patents Act 1988 or under the terms of a licence issued by the Copyright Licensing Agency Ltd, 90 Tottenham Court Road, London, England W1T 4LP. Applications for the copyright owner's written permission to reproduce any part of this publication should be addressed to the publisher.

Warning: The doing of an unauthorised act in relation to a copyright work may result in both a civil claim for damages and criminal prosecution.

The right of R.M. Simon to be identified as author of this work has been asserted by her in accordance with the Copyright, Designs and Patents Act 1988.

First published in 2005
by Jessica Kingsley Publishers
116 Pentonville Road
London N1 9JB, UK
and
400 Market Street, Suite 400
Philadelphia, PA 19106, USA

www.jkp.com

Copyright © R.M. Simon 2005

Library of Congress Cataloging in Publication Data

Simon, R. M. (Rita M.), 1921-
Self-healing through visual and verbal art therapy / R.M. Simon ; edited by S.A. Graham.
    p. cm.
  Includes bibliographical references and index.
  ISBN-13: 978-1-84310-344-8 (pbk.)
  ISBN-10: 1-84310-344-3 (pbk.)
1. Art therapy. 2. Self-care, Health. I. Title.
  RC489.A7S556 2005
  616.89'1656--dc22
                         2005003015

British Library Cataloguing in Publication Data

A CIP catalogue record for this book is available from the British Library

ISBN-13: 978 1 84310 344 8
ISBN-10: 1 84310 344 3

Printed and Bound in Great Britain by
Athenaeum Press, Gateshead, Tyne and Wear

Contents

Acknowledgements

My understanding of the therapeutic function of creative art has been immeasurably enriched by the great work of Sigmund Freud, the creator of psychoanalysis, and Donald Winnicott, psychoanalyst and paediatrician. Their writings have eventually taught me to find words to express my observations. Much that I had *seen* and recognized I was at first unable to describe for this was enacted through my patients' arts, through their paintings, writings and clay works and dramatic outbursts; all spontaneous efforts to recover themselves, surfacing into consciousness like swimmers surfacing enveloping seas.

I am very grateful to Dr Eric Strauss, Jungian analytical psychologist, who encouraged me to write about my patients' art and arranged for me to have analysis for peppercorns – a nominal fee – for some years from 1941, when I was working as a commercial artist. I am also extremely grateful to all the adult and child patients who manifest links between art and psychopathology, the comparable processes that create art and illness. Of the many who have taught me, I have especial gratitude to Dr Lovel Barnes who enabled me to experience the effectiveness of psychoanalysis; to Dr Joshua Bierer (founder of the Psychiatric Day Hospital Movement) who demonstrated the power of Adlerian social psychotherapy; to Frances Tustin, child psychotherapist, who encouraged my work in child and adolescent autism; and Marion Milner, psychoanalyst and most excellent friend.

More recently I have had fruitful discussions with Graham Music, psychoanalyst, and Alice Graham and Myriam Senez, art therapists, who have greatly helped me to arrange the book's final shape and co-ordinate the languages of art and psychoanalysis. My thanks to Kate McGrillen for typing the final manuscript.

I am continually aware how much I owe to others, to my late husband and to my children for their forbearance and help, and the many adults and children who disclose their creativity and share it with me. Last, but certainly not least, I am indebted to Joe and his mother for their positive approach and use of mental illness to confirm creativity as the source of mental health.

The Hazardous Journey

Would you come with me a hazardous journey
that might end in disaster – last too long – overshoot?
Through the smoke of my campfire a spark might fly out
as we tread through the ashes, a laughing stock?

Burning our footprints
we'd face ritual, incantation, ridicule,
Punctuation…

What sends us this hazardous journey,
far from the relative comfort
of broad backs, gloss pelts – the jostling buttocks
of herds all around us that would yet surround us?

Here wait pitfall forests and motionless lakes,
Knife-shrill birds of prey jab at our ears.
Who said we should come, anyway?

Let's face it.

Nobody gave us permission
to travel the outlands of demons,
of vampires and beautiful roses.

The Monster that waits in the bushes is howling,
His blood on the thorns of red roses falling –
'Give me your daughter, your beautiful daughter
but I will not promise to kiss or to kill her'.

When I am back where the ashes lie cold
and the rose drops its petals on the threshold,
Will you be waiting, my friend, in the grey light
or will you be far on your own inward journey?

R.M. Simon

This poem reflects an image of unthinkable anxiety as a chartless journey through the unknown to confront an ancient myth. I find myself describing Joe's drawings and stories, about Burglar Badman's journey of regression to recovery, through Freud's hypothesis of a universal unconscious myth.

Preface

Of every individual who has reached to the stage of being a unit with a limiting membrane and an outside and an inside, it can be said that there is an *inner reality* to that individual, an inner world that can be rich or poor and can be at peace or in a state of war. This helps, but is it enough? ...the third part of the life of a human being, a part that we cannot ignore, is an intermediate area of *experiencing*, to which inner reality and external life both contribute. It is an area that is not challenged, because no claim is made on its behalf except that it shall exist as a resting place for the individual engaged in the perpetual human task of keeping inner and outer reality separate yet interrelated. (Winnicott 1982, p.2)

There are some cases of art therapy that seem to epitomize the quality of this inner reality that is intensely concerned with maintaining psycho-physical health, which we may term 'self-healing' or an unconscious 'will to live' that can outreach medical expectations of a breakdown: *something enters the psyche and takes over*. Winnicott gives this something a great deal of attention, calling it *creative apperception*, saying that it is this (the mind's perception of itself) more than anything else that makes life worth living (Winnicott 1982, p.65).

I understand that our power to comprehend things creatively, to make something out of our experience is essential for maintaining mental health; however, when there is an illness there already I believe that more is needed: our creative apperception needs to become active and create something of itself – in other words, to create art as therapy.

This is not the place to discuss aesthetics but the common impulse to bring things together in a way that is individual to the creative will of the adult or child who makes something like a picture, a poem, a tune or a song.

The young boy I call Joe used his creative art to heal himself when he was in danger of becoming mentally ill. I had a small part to play in sharing his mother's concern, receiving his artwork and appreciating its importance. Living in another country I could not offer art therapy sessions so had no opportunity to see and hear his art in the process of being created; but Joe had a delusional belief that I would understand him and this was sufficient for his need. As a result, his mother and I found ourselves being used as the therapeutic container his imperative need demanded.

Now, years later, Joe and his mother have given their permission for me to publish the drawings and stories together with my interpretations of their function as spontaneous self-healing.

Introduction

> It is creative apperception more than anything else that
> makes the individual feel that life is worth living. Con-
> trasted with this is a relationship to external reality
> which is one of compliance, the world and its details
> being recognized but only as something to be fitted in
> with or demanding adaptation. (Winnicott 1982, p.65)

Winnicott believed that the creative impulse can be seen as 'a
thing in itself' (Winnicott 1982, p.69). I shall consider creative
art as a natural means of self-therapy, approaching it first in
three ways that have slowly developed in my work with adult
and child patients suffering from mental and physical illnesses:

- *first*, creativity as an *instinct*, a thing in itself
- *second*, as a *symbolic language*
- *third*, as the means of *self-healing*.

The creative instinct as a thing in itself

The delicacy of our intuitions cannot always reach beyond
conscious perception and verbal thought without the help of
psychoanalytic understanding. Two books have been especially valuable for this: *An Outline of Psychoanalysis* by Sigmund

Freud (1949a), and *Playing and Reality* by Donald Winnicott (1982).

From the various activities that we describe as instinctive, Freud hypothesizes two that are fundamental: the instinct to *create* and the instinct to *destroy*. Creation 'is to establish ever greater unities and to preserve them thus – in short, to bind together; the aim of the second, on the contrary, is to undo connections and so to destroy things' (Freud 1949a, p.6). It is not difficult to see the creative instinct in self-preservation when we are faced with a physical catastrophe. At such times we improvise to escape, to preserve self and others. But our dangers are not necessarily actual and real: we are also concerned with the internal balance between our creative and destructive impulses.

Freud supplies names for these impulses (Freud 1949a, pp.2–4). He introduced a model of personality: the blind, unconscious impulse to live he called *id*; consciousness, the intermediary between id and the external world he named the *ego*; the limitation of desire through the demands of external reality, the *superego*. Open conflict between id and superego is managed by each individual ego's power of choice, but circumstances arising from within the psyche or in outer reality can weaken the ego's power to act.

When these basic instincts manifest in art the creative instinct becomes interwoven with the destructive since we cannot create from nothing; to create we must destroy. This interweaving may be experienced as *play*, to explore with all our faculties and create new ways of living, involving the destruction of the old. Play is an instinct, but its quality depends on our attitude to life. Play can break the rules to symbolize the destructive instinct. Winnicott describes this as an achievement of creative apperception – mind's perception of itself. Thus, through play we exercise a sense of power over fate. When we create something we are relieved of the instinctual deadlock existing between id and superego, and our basic human right to compromise becomes a practical possibility.

By creating art we extend the range of the ego's potential for consciousness, the means of insight into our past and present, our inner and outer reality; outer reality can be our mental plaything, offering sameness where we had assumed difference and differences within the identical.

Winnicott, writing of patients and children, says that: '*Playing is essentially satisfying.* This is true even when it leads to a high degree of anxiety. There is a degree of anxiety that is unbearable and this destroys playing' (Winnicott 1982, p.52).

Play attracts unconscious, forgotten or repressed experiences, as well as ideas and deliberate gestures, and Marion Milner stresses the illogical quality of creative play – 'I am trying to talk about a state of mind that does in a sense stop being a state of mind as soon as we separate ourselves from it sufficiently to talk about it in logical terms' (Milner 1987, p.209).

The symbolic language of art

Play symbolizes experiences, creating its own patterns, problems and solutions, eventually establishing a particular mood. When the mood becomes visible as a drawing or painting, heard in a poem or performance, it becomes a work of art with its own aesthetic shape. Ego is strengthened by an ability to create aesthetic pleasure as a work of art but, of course, neither a real nor symbolic activity may alter any actual situation.

A work of art can be approached at two interconnected points of view, one concerned with the *subject* and the other with the *style* (or mode) of presentation. The subject matter can be discussed and its symbolism interpreted, but style seems intrinsic, demonstrating the mood or attitude shaping the artist's creative initiative. If Winnicott is right in seeing creativity as essential for mental health, the creativity that *forms an object*, as in a work of art, can become therapeutic when intolerable feelings are displaced upon it. The style reveals the artist's feelings about his or her subject.

Elsewhere I have described four basic art styles (Simon 1992, 1997). If our mind could be considered as a square room with a window on each wall, each window symbolizes a basic 'view' of life (see p.28, Figure 3.1). Two of the views are sensuous and emotional, represented by Archaic Linear and Archaic Massive styles; the other two show life through our intuitions and thoughts, represented by Traditional Massive and Traditional Linear. The space between one basic style and another, which I call transitional, can be seen in most cases as belonging to both: suggesting a continuity between the walls and views from the hypothetical room.

Visual and verbal thinking

As we continue in life we tend to be less conscious of our visual thinking and overlook its significance, relying on verbalization. Freud's description (1949b, p.22) of the essential difference between these ways of thinking substantiates my work in art therapy over more than 60 years. Freud associates visual thinking with unconscious mental functioning, and verbal thinking with articulate and, presumably, ego-organized states of mind. Verbal fluency led him to suppose that:

> Thinking in pictures is, therefore, only a very incomplete form of becoming conscious. In some way, too, it

approximates more closely to unconscious processes than does thinking in words, and it is unquestionably older than the latter... (Freud 1949b, p.23)

Creative art as self-healing

As we shall see, creative art as a means of self-healing can contain and reactivate myth in response to the destructive effects of psychic trauma. Unconscious images are pushed up like a volcanic explosion and can release the effects of trauma. Without opportunities to create something, traumatic shock may be expressed in panic or repetition-compulsion; rational thought fails to relieve the tension.

I believe that intense experiences account for the therapeutic potency of some images, poems and ageless myths, although the relevance of a particular myth may not become conscious immediately. The delicacy of visual perception is very difficult to convey in the gross structure of ordinary, or psychiatric, language. For this reason I have tried to get closer to a true presentation of the innate process that could be called *self-creation* or, alternatively, *self-healing*, drawing on psychoanalytic theory.

Psychoanalytical language extends our understanding of some unconscious factors that the artist might describe as being 'inspired'. Freud found a similar quality of apparently instinctive 'knowing':

> Some of the cultural acquisitions have undoubtedly left a deposit behind in the *id*; much of what is contributed by the super-ego will awaken an echo in the id; many of the child's new experiences will be intensified because they are repetitions of some primaeval phylogenetic experience. (Freud 1949a, p.79)

Joe's stories are first concerned with regression and later come to echo the myth of Oedipus in a truly extraordinary way, unless we can accept the idea that instinctual life has universal mental representation. Freud was convinced that 'the *archaic heritage* which a child brings with him into the world...[is] a result of the experiences of his ancestors' (Freud 1949a, p.28, emphasis added).

The creation of something tangible, such as a drawing, a game or a story, can reflect the inner imaginative reality of the creative mood seen in the outer reality of the made object. Donald Winnicott saw psychotherapy as *reflecting back* what the patient had brought: 'What Edmund did was simply to display the ideas that occupied his life. As it happened I was there mirroring whatever was taking place and thus giving it a quality of communication' (Winnicott 1982, p.43). The therapist must in fact leave room for self-healing to take place.

For Joe, his broken family would seem a total catastrophe – the loss of life's structure and meaning. His panic was expressed in crazy behaviour and a blind impulse to escape – the mindless leaping and fluttering of a bird caught in a trap. I suggested that he send me some pictures and this seemed to focus his anxiety. Freud helps me to understand how such meagre and tenuous overtures may be highly therapeutic:

> The realm of imagination was evidently a 'sanctuary' made during the painful transition from the pleasure principle to the reality principle in order to provide a substitute for the gratification of instincts which had to be given up in real life. (Freud 1948, p.118)

It appears truly remarkable that a childish fantasy could release and express emotions that had seemed altogether dissociated from rational thought, enabling art to become a natural means of self-therapy. Michael Balint clearly describes how this is seen by psychoanalysis.

> The subject is on his own and his main concern is to produce something out of himself; this something to be produced may be an object, but is not necessarily so. I propose to call this the level or area of creation. (Balint 1986, p.24)

In this particular, excited state of mind we call the creative impulse, mood appears as a pre-logical *certainty*, demanding action. The artist/child may not be able to verbalize this impulse or name the subject, but spontaneously creates its symbolic form.

Freud has described the adult artist as:

> ...like the neurotic, [he] had withdrawn from an unsatisfying reality into this world of imagination; but, unlike the neurotic, he knew how to find a way back from it and once more to get a firm foothold in reality. (Freud 1948, p.118)

Joe, like Freud's artist, found his way back through the world of imagination to firm reality.

A Brief History

Some years before she married and Joe was born, his mother had used pictorial and poetic art as a therapy; then, when Joe was seven years old, her marriage broke up in divorce.

Divorce is so common these days that the suffering of children of broken marriages may go unnoticed and even be resented if it adds to the parents' conflict and guilt. A child's confusion and fear may be overlooked, even denied a hearing.

Joe could not grasp the catastrophe that had overtaken him; he could not respond emotionally to either parent but acted with wild craziness, as if he experienced the breakdown of the family as a breakdown of reality. His mother became worried by the boy's disturbed behaviour and got in touch with me. She said that he *knew* about the divorce but he could not understand it: it made no sense to him. He became hyperactive and seemed to be without emotion.

As there was no possibility of working with her son I could only suggest that he might like to send me some drawings. From her description of his behaviour I had expected an incoherent scribble and was surprised to receive two well-organized drawings made with a red felt-tip pen.

2

Joe's Drawings

We must not be led away, in the interests of simplification perhaps, into forgetting the importance of optical
memory-residues – those of *things* (as opposed to *words*)
– or to deny that it is possible for thought-processes to
become conscious through a reversion to visual
residues, and that in many people this seems to be a
favourite method... Thinking in pictures is, therefore,
only a very incomplete form of becoming conscious. In
some way, too, it approximates more closely to unconscious processes than does thinking in words. (Freud
1949b, pp.22–3)

Joe's mother sent two drawings: one on each side of an A4
sketchbook page (they are reproduced on pages 25 and 26 at
just over half their actual size). I had hoped to get to know Joe
through his pictures and was pleased and surprised to find that
he immediately used this suggestion as a means of self-therapy.
Perhaps he had simply intended to send a stereotyped drawing
of a house that could be made quickly and easily with large
practised strokes of a red felt-tip pen, being unwilling or
unable to think about any personal matter; but Joe's creative
initiative broke through his dissociated state and he drew the
roof divided as a double pitch (see Figure 2.1).

Symbolic images reflect associations to the object for imagination extends beyond our conscious intentions. The trauma of Joe's broken home returned to consciousness in the symbolism of a house with a divided roof. His anger and fear could not be denied, but was expressed by turning the sketch over, drawing two houses, and standing near them a childlike figure together with the legend 'Burglar Badman'. At the top of the page he also wrote 'Wet pint' [*sic*] and 'Kids don't try this at home' (see Figure 2.2).

Pictorial art, however poignant, is static. Any symbolism contained in colours and tones, proportion and shape depends on the interpretation given by the observer. My interpretation may not be yours and both will depend upon our past experience; moreover we may see today what we did not see yesterday. In this cloud of associations I shall try to abstract meaning when art is to be considered as a means of therapy.

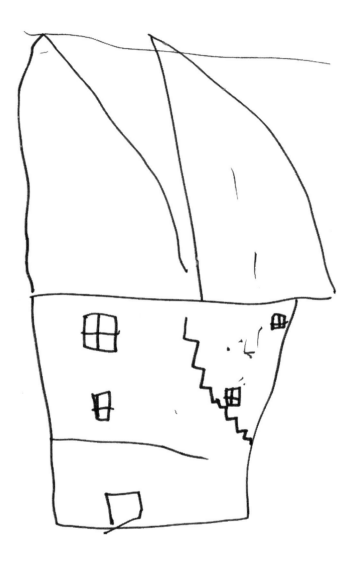

Figure 2.1 Joe's first drawing

Figure 2.2 Joe's second drawing

3

Discussion of Joe's Drawings

> It is in playing and only in playing that the individual child or adult is able to be creative and to use the whole personality, and it is only in being creative that the individual discovers the self. (Winnicott 1982, p.54)

I understand Joe's drawings as a sequence of pre-conscious thoughts that his mother's presence encouraged him to 'play' with and then express through the words which were included in the second drawing. These words provided the vehicle he needed to transfer the sensuous activity of drawing into thoughts capable of being verbalized. Because we are inclined to look first at the subject of a child's drawing or painting, its lack of representational skill may mislead us to overlook important communications that are implied in the way the artwork has been made. The meaning of the first drawing is symbolized without words but in the second drawing the meaning is divided between words and images.

By studying the *style* in relation to the *content* of Joe's pictures I came to understand his drawings as unconscious but profound statements about his life. To convey my understanding I must translate visual imagery into its verbal equivalent as far as possible and summarize my theory of art styles, which has been written in earlier books (Simon 1992, 1997).

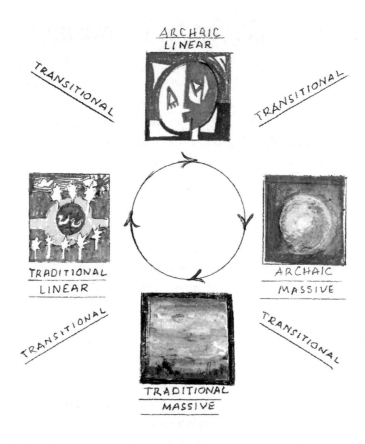

Figure 3.1 Art Styles

Joe's drawings only show two art styles, the basic Archaic Linear and a transitional style that lies between Archaic and Traditional modes (see Figure 3.1). The basic Archaic Linear is huge in scale, created by gestures of the whole arm – whatever the size of its surface area, be it notepaper or wall – while the Traditional Linear style provides the viewer with the artist's small-scale representation presenting multiple images and fine detail.

Joe's first drawing (see Figure 2.1) is typically Archaic Linear, showing his free use of the whole sheet of paper for a single image. The house appears to be drawn as a composite view showing both inside and outside, for the diagonal line on the facade seems to suggest a staircase cutting across the facade, separating two windows on the right from another pair on the left. The effect of division is enhanced by some random scribbles on the facade and roof, further emphasizing an effect of the house being in two halves.

Little children commonly identify their drawing of a house as a symbol of their family, however unconsciously: each window being associated with a member and the door standing for the dominant parent who 'holds the keys'. The facade symbolizes the family unit as if a face, expressing the artist's feelings about his home. In Joe's drawing, the facade seems to appear anxiously looking to the right, suggesting the paradoxical situation that had been hidden from him by his dissociation from the divorce that had split his home. It seemed that the act of drawing the split roof to this house made Joe conscious of the true state of things and challenged him to face the emotional impact of his broken family.

The second drawing (see Figure 2.2), made on the back of the first, is in a different mode – the transitional style between Archaic Linear and Traditional Linear. The area is now filled with a variety of images combined with words, as if Joe's visual thinking had led him to verbalize his recovered feelings. The change in style indicates a dramatic change of mood and his sensuous pleasure in making a familiar stereotyped house had developed into a complex communication.

The previous drawing (Figure 2.1) has a doorway without a door; the second drawing (Figure 2.2) faces the fact that his divided home has two houses, each with a single, lopsided roof and a door with a window in it. These houses are not identical and the red felt-pen line leads and follows Joe's feeling about their difference. We follow his thought through their differ-ence in scale, placement and quality of line (Kellogg 1970). Joe would have been taught to write from the top, left-hand side of the paper so we might assume that he first placed a house on the left and the other at the bottom on the right sym-bolizing a final statement, or full stop.

When we compare the lines shaping these houses, the house on the left is taller and its outline indicates that originally Joe intended it to be taller still. A fluid, lightly-drawn outline envelops four windows and a central door with a window in it drawn as firmly as is the asymmetrical roof. This house empha-sizes its role as an enclosure but the outline is indecisive, more like the outline of a face than a building: the top windows (as eyes in the face-facade) seem to look to the right and the door (as a mouth) might be half open.

The house at the bottom of the paper is four-square and compact, with two windows in the middle, one clearly drawn and the other contracted as if by crossed glazing bars. Two more windows are crammed under the line of the eaves and a rather misshapen door is half crossed by awkward glazing bars; as a 'house-face' its facade appears to scowl.

The transitional style, indicating a modification of both visual and verbal expression, seems focused on a little figure extensively scribbled over with the red pen who commands the centre of the picture. Its proportions are of a child of about two, who faces us straight-forward, a little to the right of centre, his face turned somewhat right and the right arm half-raised from the elbow, the left arm reaching straight down. Head, mouth and body are crudely scribbled over and the eyes crossed out. Both feet are carefully drawn and turned to the left beside a scrawl that looks like a signature.

The manikin stands stiffly – even the mouth is shut away beneath the scribble. Yet two lines have escaped to the right, one from the mouth that ends in a spiral like a shout. The other moves, either from the mouth or up the half-lifted arm, to an open shield-like shape that is diagonally bisected; one half containing a tiny, house-like shape and the other a crossed and scribbled circle.

What is this little character? As we study it, the more complex it seems. Who is he? He cannot see or speak, the eyes behind the line are blank, the head appears to be capped and hooded, his cranium attacked with scribble.

Symbolism

It is easy to play with ideas about the little figure, especially when it has been drawn on a piece of paper, but it is difficult for a thinking adult to grasp how fast and economic is the fantasy that lies behind such an image. No wonder that its detail could be overlooked or dismissed as accidental. It is only when we look at Joe's drawing with as much attention to its symbolism as we would give to the grammar and syntax of words that we can reach towards the mental processes of visual thought.

Joe's change of style between the two drawings gives a clue to his change of mood if we accept the idea that free drawings, like free associations, symbolize repressed and unconscious emotions before they have been coloured and shaped into verbal thought. For instance, three circles are placed on the upper part of the drawing, the largest circle crossed with one filled-in segment. Another, smaller circle holds an inverted triangle that is scribbled over and the third circle is minute, containing a cross. Abstract symbols provide a link between visual and verbal art, their meaning being half in the content and half in their shape, a circle being a symbol of the Whole Self – of universal significance (Jung 1967, p.222) – and also 'a limiting membrane with an outside and an inside' (Winnicott 1982, p.2).

I recognize the visual thinking that finally became conscious and available to verbal thought, naming the figure as 'Burglar Badman' and extending his idea about the image's threatening appearance, writing in green felt-pen 'Wet pint'[sic]. Then, perhaps as an afterthought, adding a pencilled warning: 'Kids don't try this at home'. As he wrote it seemed that the shock edged further into consciousness until visual representation overcame his repression, approaching consciousness directly:

> Actually the difference is that, whereas with uncon-
> scious *ideas* connecting links must be forged before
> they can be brought into the consciousness, with
> *feelings*, which are themselves transmitted directly, there
> is no necessity for this. In other words: the distinction
> between conscious and pre-conscious has no meaning
> where feelings are concerned…feelings are either con-
> scious or unconscious. Even when they are connected
> with verbal images, their becoming conscious is not

due to that circumstance, but they become so directly. (Freud 1949b, p.26)

A mood as seen in an artwork is linked to, or coloured by, an underlying attitude to life. Many years spent studying art styles justify my assumption that a drawing style tells us an artist's present attitude to life (Simon 1992, 1997). The Archaic Linear indicates a sensuous approach, the Archaic Massive an emotional attitude, both dominated by subjective experience. The Traditional Massive and Linear styles refer to the external world and reflect in turn intuition and thought. Study of archaic and traditional art forms, whether by adults or children, amateurs or professionals from the present or ancient world, reflect *any* of the four basic art styles. Joe, as any other seven-year-old, used an archaic style and had not yet fully developed a traditional mode of representation. A change from one style to another indicates his change of mood, as Joe's second drawing anticipated a return to verbal thinking and communication skill. Regression in an art style is a particularly important indication or anticipation of change that may be pathological or therapeutic such as 'a regression in service of the ego' (Kris 1973, p.177).

Although I had not been able to watch Joe making the drawings, both subject and style gave me a good idea of the visual thinking that accompanied them: I was impressed by his flexibility of mood, showing that he had found 'the facilitating environment' (Winnicott 1982, p.66) needed for psychic change. This facilitating environment was provided by his mother's acceptance of his need for therapeutic regression.

Joe did not send any more drawings but, for whatever reason, changed his art form, dictating stories for his mother to send me at intervals.

4

Comparing Visual and Verbal Imagery

As babies we expressed our sensations, long before we could speak, through sounds and random gestures that were later largely replaced by words. Our earliest drawing, expressed as scribbling, displayed the sensuous pleasure of marking any receptive surface. The gestures that accidentally formed circles and other enclosing shapes soon attract the attention of a child from 12 months, leading to deliberate repetition and formation as a container. *The Symbolism of Style* (Simon 1992) contains detailed descriptions of these first drawings. The circle becomes a first symbolic image of 'me', followed by the gradual separation of 'my parts' and differentiation of them; thus 'me' can become 'my'. In time this closed shape becomes associated with the idea of a face, then a body attached to it that invites the young artist to identify circles with a combined 'Self/Other' of faces, legs and arms that can be repeated endlessly as the ubiquitous 'man' (Kellogg 1970).

Between drawing and writing lies an area of mental life that allows recollection to be played with. Freud described this area of fantasy as 'pre-conscious' (Freud 1949b, p.32). When adults and children draw freely in an apparently thoughtless or aimless way, ideas occur from their unconscious associations to the lines and shapes. Joe's dissociated feelings had blocked such creative play until he had drawn a stereotyped house that symbolized his family, with his father as the huge incomplete roof.

Winnicott describes the pathological aspect of fantasying as opposed to dreaming: 'Dream fits into object-relating in the real world... By contrast, however, fantasying remains an isolated phenomenon, absorbing energy but not contributing-in either to dreaming or to living' (Winnicott 1982, p.26).

In this case Joe's fantasy could not undo the reality of the divorce but it released his blocked emotion and he became conscious of the destructive rage that had been hidden away in crazy hyperactivity fitting nowhere; as dreams, his drawings and stories are 'object-relating to the real world'.

However, I find that when fantasy *develops* as a story or a painting/drawing (with a beginning, middle and end) it becomes a work of art as part of the external reality. This happened for Joe when he moved beyond visual symbolism and his fantasy could be developed as a myth. These stories provided a means for his mother to join him in the fantasy, as she wrote to his dictation.

5

Joe's Stories

The stories continue the self-therapy that began when he drew a house with a strange divided roof. This broke through a dissociation that had blocked off violent feelings of outrage caused by his parents' divorce.

Joe's feelings were too powerful to be contained in ordinary childish misbehaviour. However, the second drawing had enabled him to verbalize his distress, making a therapeutic regression (Kris 1973, p.177) through the destructive image of Burglar Badman which later led to a correlation in the positive image of young Danny.

He told seven stories; much later he wrote one more for himself.

The first story of Burglar Badman

There was a dog, he barked a lot and barked so much that he ripped all the books into smithereens. And the bad man robber came to the house and he couldn't find anything but ripped paper – and he said 'What am I going to get from this house? I know.' Suddenly the policeman jumped out on the burglar bad man and said 'You are under arrest for eating your dad's vest and you broke the wool, the British Bulldog wool' and he coughed a lot that he made the house get all covered in dog's droppings. And it was very stupid of him. He was prosecuted and broke all his broken stuff even more, he was that cross.

The burglar forgot that he broke a small window and he said 'Oh dear. I better get this fixed.' So he got all the broken bits and threw it on and then he got some putty and put it on and said 'There it's as good as new, and I can go home and see what I have robbed and maybe break some of the stuff and see if I can fix them again too and give them back.'

So he fixed them and gave them back and then when he got out and gave them their robberies back. And he was so silly that he didn't notice a policeman coming out on me and was so silly that he put his hat on and his stuff on and pretended that he was the dog who broke all the things and covered the house with dog's droppings. And he put on the TV to see what was on but there wasn't nothing except a blank screen. And he said 'Oh well, I'd better go home and get some more robberies and maybe break them again. I'm a really silly burglar. I want to get arrested for doing all that silliness and maybe smash the policeman and fix them again.'

Discussing this story

Health can be looked at in terms of fusion (erotic and destructive drives) and this makes more urgent than ever the examination of the origin of aggression and of destructive fantasy. (Winnicott 1982, p.70)

The first story moves from the negative primary instinct of destruction, as symbolized by the dog, to expression of anger at his father's destruction of the secure home. This is so intolerable to Joe that he has to wipe out memory of the good father/male element as depicted in the reliable square house in the second drawing. Therefore I find the main theme is the therapeutic development from *instinct* to *ambivalence* (breaking and mending) aroused by *emotion*. The father/male element is seen to be taking the blame. At this time the mother/female element is ignored, because of the danger in consciously hating his mother – she might also leave. In this story we find the creative instinct bonded to its opposite, and Joe's instinctive reaction to his parents' divorce is reflected in the destructive behaviour of the dog who tears up all the papers and books that symbolize knowledge. The dog cannot speak but barks and barks until his place can be taken by an articulate badman robber who is then confronted by the police.

I interpret this, the split in Joe's psyche, as the conflict between Joe's *id* in the shape of a dog, and the *ego* as Burglar Badman, whose lawlessness and stupidity is arrested by the *superego* as the police. The ego wonders what he gets from such destruction and apparently has the answer – 'I know' – but this insight also is 'arrested'. 'You are under arrest for eating your dad's vest and you broke the wool, the British Bulldog wool.'

I consider this to symbolize his unconscious desires for fusion with the father. Symbolism is inclusive carrying the proviso 'and, and, and' that may be loosely attached to words as part of primary mental processes described by Freud (1949a, p.25); for a symbol's subjective meaning is perpetually innovative and mutable. Therefore opposites can be fused. 'Dad's vest' includes both love of the father *and* patricide; also the wider issue concerning infant fantasy of incest. However, these feelings are not acceptable to consciousness; he is caught out and has to 'cough up' because at this time he cannot restore his post-Oedipal love towards his father.

The fantasy of symbolic incest with the father points to emotions occurring in earliest childhood when erotic feelings were moving between male and female objects: thus establishing Joe's identification with the absent father as the betrayer of his family and giving freedom for this fantasy. This may also account for the Badman's persistent indecision in breaking and repairing. However, Joe's will is not so easily subdued and the ensuing struggle between ego and id is continued in the anal sadism of the shitting dog and the breaking and mending of a window. Ambivalence continues to destroy his attempts at making reparation.

Joe's attention is distracted from external reality and his sense of being 'cut off' is symbolized by the blank TV screen and failure to notice and maintain a defence against the policeman/superego coming out on him. The screen and the disguises can be seen as evasions, not acknowledging hatred of the parents who have destroyed his reality. Joe admits to pretence: a conscious split in his psyche recognizes the pretence of dressing up, and being a dog to release his animal sadism. Finally, he as superego can admit he is 'a really silly burglar'. However, it would appear that he immediately abandons this insight for he continues by partially identifying with the Badman. Equivocalness bedevils the story throughout. However, Joe must have been delighted with the story for he signed it with a flourish.

I see the symbolic regression that Joe had to take to recover a sense of the emotional reality of his life as an unhappy child.

His inability to accept this reality had endangered his mental health but his inherent creativity led him to make drawings and stories through which he could heal himself. Creativity does not distinguish between fantasies of progression and regression; here and in three more stories Joe expresses his regression as extreme ambivalence.

The second story

Burglar Badman went into a house and there was a lot of food so he ate all of it. He had a very sore stomach so he went over to a police station and smashed some police. That made him happy. And he said 'I am going to start being badder, and I am going to smash some policemen.' Then he smashed some policemen and he had a victory for the day. But the police were still after him, he didn't care. More like the police cared a lot.

Then he became badder. He went on TV. Then the policewoman came to mark him out. He was a terrible man.

Discussing this story

Conscious processes on the periphery of the ego, and everything else in the ego unconscious – such would be the simplest state of affairs that we might picture. And such may in fact be the conditions prevailing in animals. But in men there is an added complication owing to which internal processes in the ego may also acquire the quality of consciousness. This complication is produced by the function of speech, which brings the material in the ego into a firm connection with the memory-traces of visual and more particularly of auditory perceptions. (Freud 1949a, p.22)

Joe's hyperactivity and craziness seem to have been the result of ungovernable anxiety that was relieved when he was able to symbolize his feelings. This creative work, appreciated by his mother as 'drawings' and a 'story', transferred his chaotic anger and fear into the structure of a myth, where the hero was a badman. But the original drawing had only shown a tiny, rigid child shouting or screaming. 'The id contains everything that is inherited…fixed in the constitution – above all therefore the instincts' (Freud 1949a, p.2).

This second, brief story again releases the Badman from the rigidity of the drawing. First, it symbolizes his outrage as a failure of nurture, for although there is a lot of food, he gets a sore stomach. He cannot digest the good sustenance his home provides. 'And for however long a child is fed at his mother's breast, he will always be left with a conviction after he is weaned that his feeding was too short and too little' (Freud 1949a, pp.56–7).

He then reacts by attacking the police, so the second story is also free to regress and play 'let's pretend' (no longer completely identifying with the dog), for the Badman as the id decides to 'start being badder and…smash some policemen'. He now can display himself on TV in the guise of a terrible man (real play acting) and this gives him victory for a day – until the ego intervenes as a policewoman.

If policemen symbolize Joe's 'male element' and the policewoman his 'bisexual aspect' of latency (Winnicott 1982, pp.76–84), we can assume that his sense of self felt threatened by both police forces in conflict within the superego. The little boy defies the policeman (father) until the policewoman (mother) comes to 'mark him out'. The female element, which was ignored in the first story, now takes over from the played-out male element.

The usefulness of these stories as part of therapy is that a quality of fiction is allowed to surround and express deep hopes and fears that otherwise would be completely identified with.

The third story

One day Burglar Badman found a house. He smashed the window and he went inside. He fixed the window and he smashed the door window after he went to another house, and then he found a lady crying. He said 'What's wrong you stupid?' Then he said 'I look pretty good, don't I? Couldn't I be your boyfriend for as long as I live?' He said 'Do you love me?' and she said 'For certain, not.' Then he said 'My suit looks rather funny, doesn't it? Come on, let's go out and see if there is a church open so we can get married. Pretty nice, huh? You must marry me. If you say I'm not going to marry you I will smash you.' He said 'You look stupid. I must get a groom suit.' And she got one, he said 'That's not good enough, that looks stupid. Go out again and find a proper one with a shawl and you look beautico da tutti. You're beautiful but I'm not going to marry you so just put that stupid suit back, you stupid shit. You're lovely.' He says 'Because you look stupid I love you and I hate you. You are a little bit of this and a little bit of that. I love you but I hate you now. My sack looks

great and so does your horrible face. You look
like the grand high witch of the witches. You are
stupid 'cos I love you. You look lovely 'cos you're
stupid, 'cos I think you look lovely and that's the
end. But you look lovely but you don't change
out of that. Are you ready to get married, now?
But the only thing is that I'm a burglar and you
can be one too with me and that's the end. You
are my wife now.'

Discussing this story

The dominant theme of this long story is overriding ambivalence towards every aspect. The story shows us the complexity,
the displacement and condensation possible to symbolic
thought (Freud 1949a, pp.29–36). Joe's first concern is with
his divided home and we are shown his feelings about his
parents through the symbolism of two houses. He smashed a
window and went inside to mend it, then he smashes a door
window when he had gone inside another house, where he
finds a lady crying. I find Joe's windowed door ambivalent,
both a barrier and an entrance, its window offering insight, a
way to see the outer world and inside the building. An attack
on its windows would weaken the ego in its task as 'mediator'
between inner and outer reality. Nevertheless, the door that has
a window in it is important to Joe's myth. It is a complex
symbol that we might read as an ego with power to let in and
keep out the id. Having a window in the door implies the
power of insight that allows this barrier (door) to be seen
through from either side.

I see the crying lady as a symbol of his dissociated female
self whose mourning for the lost mother cannot be borne, but
must be negatively projected as he finds the lady 'stupid'.

Symbols give life to unconscious processes which we consider as primary (Freud 1949a, p.25); the meanings we ascribe to them are drawn from many circumstances that, for lack of evidence, we can only guess. Freud, interpreting these processes symbolized in dreams, explains that: 'contraries are not kept apart from each other but are treated as though they were identical, so that in the manifest dream any element may also stand for its contrary' (Freud 1949a, p.31). An unconstrained picture or a story has the same quality of primary processes, and I must pick my way through numerous possibilities to find interpretations that seem to explain the fact of Joe's spontaneous recovery.

The symbolism of two houses and two windows in this story depends upon a contrast between the two houses seen in the Burglar Badman drawing. The ovoid house without a door, or the means of opening and closing it, and the other house that is barred can only be entered by breaking a window which the Badman must then repair. The two houses symbolize the parents – one being shut away from him (the father) and the other defenceless like a crying woman. He is threatened by this call upon his sympathy. This is intolerable to him, as he *needs* to be a Burglar Badman in order to regress. He insults her, while demanding total submission in married love. Joe continues to pursue his desire for narcissistic satisfaction but his ambivalence again defeats him; he is tormenting and tormented by love and hate, a need for both unity and revenge, so he then tries to compromise with 'a little bit of this and a little bit of that'.

Winnicott's description of male and female elements in boys and girls (Winnicott 1982, pp.72–85) helps us to understand Joe's conflict as being between his female need to *be* and his male need to *do* and *be done to* – the eternal conflict between the individual and society (the police). In this dilemma we also need to follow the complications of psychic splitting between Badman, Joe's ego and his id; it is almost as if the story has three people to deal with!

The first is the Badman as a regression from the Oedipal situation. The second is the ego, weakened by the shock of the divorce, which cannot resolve this ambivalence and mends the window. Torn between love and hate Joe's ego must act as 'intermediary between the id and the external world' (Freud 1949a, p.2). The ego breaks in to speak through the lady when the Badman asks if she loves him, and she calmly replies, 'For certain, not.'

The third split is by the id, the instinct for destruction that becomes sufficiently conscious to break the windows and insult the lady. We have already heard the equable voice of ego describe the Badman as a very silly burglar, but ego is too weak to respond to the lady's grief, while the id remains lost in admiration for itself and determined to possess the lady. The Badman wants a conventional marriage, all the trappings, the groom suit and the dress with a shawl, but the lady has not agreed to love the id. She quietly preserves her identity when the id can only see her as 'the grand high witch of the witches' and 'a stupid shit'.

The rational ego tries to find a reason for the lady's reticence – perhaps it is because he is a burglar? So the id insists that she can be a burglar; he then loses patience and says, 'that's the end. You are my wife now'.

The fourth story

One day Burglar Badman he went and said to the police, 'If you keep me in prison for life I will smash you. You look stupid and you are a silly

plonker'. The Badman said 'What's wrong? Shall I
fix you up again'. And they said 'We'll fix ourself
up'. Once the police had him in jail for 15 years
and he smashed them and he didn't fix them up,
so he and they threw the key down the drain and
he said 'Hey. Good job.' Then he found a girlfriend and he said 'I love you and I will never say I
hate you because you are just a beautiful old
plonker. I'll have you in my sandwiches. You are a
good compadre. Would you let me escape and
would you promise and keep your promise to let
me stay out and I wouldn't be a baddy and I
would be a baddy. He calls himself Peter so they
say you compadre.' The next day he said 'I've got
a name for you. Burglaranna man. You are a nice
woman so I will use you for my Staff. You look
like a tramp and you are a guacamole. You are
stupid. You should have looked like me and my
Staff. Compadre, you look like an egg in a slicer.
You're a great little woman 'cos you think I'm
lovely and I think you're lovely too and I am
lovely. So I must say you are are a plonker. A
beautiful honeybunch. Now I think you look
Butico da Tutti. And you must start from scratch.
A nice woman.'

Discussing this story

The fourth story presents the critical stage of Joe's regression to
basic instincts of creation and destruction and to the oral
component of psychosexual development, before a return to
emotions typical of the seven-year-old boy. We have followed
Joe's regressive fantasies and tolerated with him their weak-

ening effect on his ego. His emerging creativity again takes us beyond his pictorial image of a rigid little warrior but we did not expect to find so swift a change in his newly restored emotions.

I find this story to be the symbolic *process* by which Joe was able to resolve infantile conflicts about his parents, couched in the jargon of a schoolboy who is in the latency (dormant) period of psychosexual development (Freud 1949a, p.11). Because Joe had been able to regress so deeply in his stories he could visualize thoughts that a baby might have but be unable to verbalize. However, thanks to this monologue, I was able to pick out the elements of mood change from id to ego by collecting together the ways that Joe regarded the male and female elements in himself, as they were symbolized in the changing way he saw the police and the lady.

We recall that in the first story the dog was seen as a projection of id's destructiveness (books) towards the superego/police. But now Joe is beginning to be reconciled through the symbol of the police, first smashed, then seen as sharing responsibility with the Badman by throwing away the key. When the police say, 'We'll fix ourself up', is not Joe recognizing the hypocrisy of his offer to do this for them?

Having accepted a more positive male aspect he can then see the female as a girlfriend rather than a lady. Joe's projection of the female aspect of his personality, previously a despised lady, now creates this girlfriend, a step in detaching himself from his denigrated female element. But, trying to evade his destructiveness, he is caught in ambivalence. Although he promises, 'I will never say I hate you', oral sadism takes over, his promise is overswept and he concludes '…you are just a beautiful old plonker. I'll have you in my sandwiches'.

The Badman turns to his ego (female aspect) to admit the need for help; Joe cries, 'Would you let me escape and would you promise and keep your promise to let me stay out and I wouldn't be a baddy', but id is too strong, overpowers him and concludes, 'I would be a baddy.' After this failure it looks as if Joe had reverted to deception for he calls himself Peter so that they will call him 'compadre'; but the next day he has a new plan. The girl should have looked like the Badman and then she could have joined his staff as a bisexual Burglaranna man.

I imagine that Joe hoped that this deception would relieve the pain of his resistance to the female element by making her almost entirely male, a false solution that Winnicott describes (saying to his male patient): 'I am listening to a girl. I know perfectly well that you are a man but I am listening to a girl, and I am talking to a girl' (Winnicott 1982, p.73).

When Joe abandons this idealistic hope to the deepest regression of oral sadism – 'I'll have you in my sandwiches' – this expression of his destructiveness makes the idea fully conscious and brings the opposite in its wake. We know that a hateful and vengeful mood can 'turn into' the expression and release of positive feeling: that destruction is allied to creation. Suddenly it seems as if the war is over, the sky clears, the regression is played out and Joe's female element as ego-ideal has become a great little *woman* 'cos you think I'm lovely and I think you're lovely and I am lovely'. Speaking for himself Joe says to the Badman and the woman, 'you must start from scratch'.

I am very much aware of the clumsiness of logical interpretation:

We have no way of conveying knowledge of a complicated set of simultaneous processes except by describing them successively; and thus it happens that all our accounts err in the first instance in the direction of one-sided simplification and must wait till they can be supplemented, reconstructed and so set right. (Freud 1949a, p.77)

It is difficult for the logical mind to follow a symbolism that allows for the particular nature of primary process thinking, condensations and displacement, as in the language of dreams. How far can Joe trust the Badman now that the Badman and the police are side by side throwing the key down the drain? Can Joe hope to sustain a truce between his creative and destructive instincts through homosexual love of Burglaranna man and, when adult, transfer his desire for the lady to the more appropriate image of a girl? Can changing his name to Peter turn a Badman into a Goodman? Surely Joe's peace of mind depends upon a strengthened ego and a return to the everyday world of the seven-year-old child he had lost to regression. Is he now ready to deal with the *reality* of post-Oedipal hating and loving and being loved?

The fifth story – Burglar Badman gets a job

One day Burglar Badman became no more bad. He did no more crimes. He got a job in a Whole Food shop. He saw a stick of liquorice and somebody asked for a special offer from Burglar Goodman. He said 'Certainly.' 'Thank you very much, Burglar Goodman' said the man. His name was Ryan. 'It is now time to find out who said the answer of the crimes that Burglar Goodman had done so far.' Then that day a strange man said 'GIVE ME YOUR MONEY OR YOUR LIFE.' The End.

Discussing this story

'The sole quality that rules in the id is that of being uncon-scious. Id and unconscious are as intimately united as ego and pre-conscious' (Freud 1949a, p.23). If we choose to see Joe's stories as part of a myth we can see Burglar Badman as an embodiment of the destructive instinct, split off from its creative component by the demands of sensuous life. Free from emotional judgements of right and wrong Joe could express his almost unbridled fantasies, normally belonging in unconscious mental life, except when symbolized in dreams. But Joe chan-nelled the urgent need to deal with his trauma into acceptable communication and his mother gave him the incentive to create. In the time that was essential for holding his excited, frightened state Joe had reached back in three stories to the 'raging baby' of the second drawing. But in the fourth story the myth had disappeared, the lady was replaced by a girl*friend* and the heartless Badman began to find that he was loveable. Myth has no truck with facts, hopes and promises. Given these, it dissolves into a fairy tale.

In this, the fifth story, Badman now as Goodman goes to work for *whole* food in a shop. Surely this is Joe's ego-ideal – 'the self's conception of how he wishes to be' (Rycroft 1972, p.45). Kind, generous, polite, this shopkeeper can give away liquorice to a man called Ryan who is polite in return. When the Badman finds himself loved and loving he reaches the phallic stage of sexual development and attempts to enter the adult world of shopkeeping.

The first and most important thing we observe is Joe's change of mood. The first four stories have been highly ambiv-alent. Now his mood is much more detached and he tells us about people in the outer world, as when Badman becomes a shopkeeper. It would seem there is a real change of attitude towards his inner world with a greatly strengthened ego and a will to understand. I imagine that Joe, as Ryan, wants 'the answer of the crimes' – he wants to understand his myth: who the Badman was and what happened to love and truth during his regression?

However, ego control is temporarily blocked when a stranger intervenes and Joe's ego has to withdraw, surrendering to the id. If the stranger is interpreted as a primitive superego, Joe is forced to feel shame and guilt. And if he faces this insight he could come to terms with the Badman's activities, but at this time Joe's ego was not capable of facing this task.

In Winnicott's terms: 'It is rewarding to view one's current clinical material keeping in mind this one example of dissociation, the split-off girl element in a male patient' (Winnicott 1982, p.77). The Goodman had recovered the object and meets the difficulty of object relating to his female element. I see this in the fact that there are no women around when the Goodman is keeping shop, for it must have been difficult for Joe to work with the phallic stage in his stories at a time when he depended on his mother to act as his secretary. It speaks much for her forbearance during this phase.

The sixth story – Lipstick

The Lipstick story is all about a wee boy. One day there was this wee boy, and his name was Danny. And his girlfriend had lipstick. And the problem with lipstick with Danny was it smelt funny when it got old.

The little boy hated lipstick, was a dipstick whenever it was old. Then Danny had a brain wave. He said to his girlfriend 'I hope you never, ever again wear lipstick.' The End.

Discussing this story

Around this time Joe's creativity had seemed to pause and when I received a story called 'Lipstick' I found that the Goodman had been replaced by a wee boy called Danny who meets his female element on the new ground of relationship. The story presented a considerable shift in the relation of id to ego that allowed for the rational mood we associate with mental health. As Winnicott says, if we see health as a fusion between creation and destruction, we need to understand the origin of aggressive and destructive fantasies (Winnicott 1982, p.70).

We have followed Joe's id in its concern to defend itself through destructive and sadistic behaviours that became modified when the Badman lost sight of the lady and acquired a girlfriend. When the Goodman gets a job in the shop, Joe's female element has seemed in abeyance; there is no sign of a girlfriend in this commercial world inhabited by males.

I see this as the critical moment in Joe's story that might have been the end of it, as well as the end of the Goodman, but Joe's creative initiative led him into a world that was much closer to the everyday. The Badman vanishes, the compromise with Goodman has failed and Goodman, Ryan and the stranger have been dealt with – an unsatisfactory situation but inevitable in the circumstances. I had the satisfaction of knowing that Joe's ego had resisted the regressive pull of the id and his creativity was intact with this story about Danny, a wee boy like Joe himself, who is closer to actual reality.

The first aspect of the Lipstick story is the way in which Joe's ego has 'settled down' to mediate between id and super-ego and allow for more realistic expectations. Then he can persuade his girlfriend to give up the remnants of the primary object as symbolized by the out-of-date lipstick. He persuades her courteously by saying that he *hopes* she will never ever use lipstick again! The strength of his restored ego is shown in the protracted nature of hope. This would allow Joe (as the female element girlfriend) to relinquish primary love and be free to develop other relationships.

Joe has begun to establish ego control and wants to bring this into line with the ego-ideal of an all-wise adult. However, he is also mindful of the outer reality of Danny as a wee boy and must separate the ego-ideal from an outmoded Oedipal attachment to his mother.

Art is a mirror of the world as experienced by the artist's mood and therefore extends logical self-comprehension towards hope; Danny could have a 'brain wave' that takes him beyond Joe's immediate capacity for rational thought. Joe's story strives towards objectivity and manages a phobic response to the oral sadism it threatened to re-evoke; ego makes a firm stand against 'all lipstick'. His strengthened ego is successful, regression is left behind and the primary processes of thought that accompany it have given way to secondary elaborations from external reality. When the balance between id, ego and superego became adjusted to normal lines, we see that Joe's stories, developed with the barbaric simplicity of myth, have changed to fairy tales. The Badman had become a boy, the mythic lady a girl, and the terrifying stranger a brain wave.

Winnicott describes normal development in children:

> In so far as the individual boy or girl has now reached to personal organisation of inner psychic reality, this inner reality is constantly being matched with samples of external or shared reality. A new capacity for object relating has now developed, namely, one that is based on an interchange between external reality and samples from the personal psychic reality. This capacity is

reflected in the child's use of symbols and in creative playing and, as I have tried to show, in the gradual ability of the child to use cultural potential in so far as it is available in the immediate social environment. (Winnicott 1982, p.131)

When Joe tells us that the wee boy Danny hates old lipstick, I think that he is working through the trauma of his parents' broken marriage, through its disturbing effect upon the Oedipus complex. This time round Joe's creative initiative has an elegant flash of intuition, a 'brain wave' that a moderate request will release his girlfriend from this Oedipal bond. However, Oedipus would have to leave his kingdom; blinded, he would take the lonely course that seems the death of hope.

The seventh story – Part two of 'Lipstick'

She, the girlfriend of Danny, died one day and Danny was crying every day of his life and he just had to get on with his own life. One day he cried for an hour and five minutes, he was so upset about his girlfriend's death. Danny decided to do something about it so it would seem very funny because he would tell his mummy what happened about a year ago, when he was 20. The End.

A year ago, when he was 20, his girlfriend died.

Discussing this story

Although it seems that Joe had intended to end his story with Danny's rational management of his lipstick phobia, this could not be sustained. Joe could not give up primary love without the complementary instinct for destruction being activated. In

An Outline of Psychoanalysis, Freud refers to the conflict between the basic instincts.

> We may picture an initial state of things by supposing that the whole available energy of Eros [libido]…is present in the as yet undifferentiated ego-id and serves to neutralize the destructive impulses which are simultaneously present… So long as that [destructive] instinct operates internally, as a death instinct, it remains silent; we only come across it when it becomes diverted outwards as an instinct of destruction. (Freud 1949a, p.7)

Joe's creative initiative continued to use his female element (girlfriends) to neutralize his destructiveness. Earlier, under the influence of the id, its negative image had been projected upon the lady, but when the Burglar was threatened by the stranger the self-destructive impulse could be contained because his ego had strengthened. So in the seventh story there was nothing else for it: the girlfriend must die. In spite of his unwillingness to face the inevitable, Joe struggles to distinguish past from present when he says: 'A year ago, when he was 20, his girlfriend died.' Surely this must indicate a more sufficient ego control in his growing ability to separate past and present.

Guilt is almost overwhelming: Danny cries every day of his life until his suffering forces Joe to reconsider his position. Klein describes this normal stage of sensibility in childhood as *the depressive position* (Klein 1940, pp.125–53) that each individual works through in ways that accord with component factors, such as their inborn aggressiveness and the relative strength of the ego. Prior to the family breakdown we presume Joe had dealt with the Oedipus complex and embarked upon the depressive position but the ensuing trauma forced him to regress – 'a regression in service of the ego' (Kris 1973, p.177). The girl must be given up as incestuous wishes must be if we are to live a normal life and the image of the actual mother must be separated from the Oedipal fantasies as asserted by Klein. His achievement of mental health demanded that he work through the Oedipal state to consciously acknowledge his experience of loss and bereavement.

With extraordinary insight Joe consciously decides to do something about it and plans his defence against his suffering. Joe's ego strength and understanding seem almost incredible in the plan to cultivate the manic defence as a deliberate version of his dissociated state; Danny will make it seem very funny and this will sustain him until he is sufficiently adult to discuss these feelings with his mother.

Then Joe indicates that his anxiety and pain have exhausted him; he announces the end of the story, but he cannot yet let go until he has reiterated her death.

He seems to feel some confusion about claiming author-ship for, when he had signed the story, he then wrote '*is that od by...*'(Odd Boy) and added his mother's name. I think that this indicates his awareness of the compulsive nature of the creative drive that extends beyond will to achieve the image of psychic integration. We remember that Joe was dictating for his mother to write, and here he was now acknowledging her part in bringing fantasy into the reality of a story. I see his footnote as another indication of his return to the everyday world that censors admissions by the id. This is an important indicator of difference between primary and secondary processes of think-ing and a guide to a need to change – in Joe's case to refer to the mores of external reality. It shows me that he was aware of *com-municating* to someone, an inner self that might have been trans-ferred upon 'his mother's friend'. This aspect of the creative instinct had not been apparent when he only needed to communicate to himself.

Michael Balint writes well of this in his discussion of the area of creation:

> ...there is no external object present. The subject is on his own and his main concern is to produce something out of himself; this something to be produced may be an object, but is not necessarily so. I propose to call this the level or area of creation. The most often discussed example is, of course, artistic creation, but other phenomena belong to the same group, among them mathematics and philosophy, gaining insight, understanding something or somebody; and last, but not least, two highly important phenomena: the early phases of becoming – bodily or mentally – 'ill' and spontaneous recovery from an 'illness'.
>
> We know that there are no 'objects' in the area of creation, but we know also that for most – or some – of the time the subject is not entirely alone there. (Balint 1986, pp.24–5)

I understand Joe's 'area of creation' to have been induced when he became absorbed in drawing the distorted house that released him from his dissociation and I assume that his mother's help was invaluable for communicating the Badman, whom Joe had discovered in his second drawing.

This is an example of the difference between visual and verbal thinking. Communication through visual symbols remains subjective but gains a measure of objective reality when a meaning can be put into words. Michael Balint is concerned here with the development in a mood of formless creativity towards psychoanalytic understanding, through the creation of a *communicating object* (a work of art or science) that is essential if we are to distinguish fantasy from delusion or hallucination.

It is obvious that the gap between fantasy and reality is bridged when a work of art is made, then recognized and appreciated by someone other than its creator. This brings me to the point of saying that Joe's instinct to create enabled him to make the link between sanity and madness that is art. Creative art can make possible the conscious appreciation of unconscious content. The 'gap' between these opposites is the cultural defence against delusion that must be managed if any new creation is to be generally understood.

The eighth story – Burglar Badman

One day the burglar decided to do a mugging in the street, but in the end he decided it wasn't fair to hurt someone old. So he decided to keep with house robbery BUT ONE THING HE COULD NEVER KEEP WAS A FAMILY. He could take money, TVs, stereos, but all he could GET was years in prison.

He was trying to keep clean but it was hard. He decided to call his friends but they got executed for carrying nine million dollars of cocaine through Thailand. He decided to spend some money on expensive wine and spent 60 dollars on it.

Burglar Badman's false driving licence was found. He decided to call himself a fake name, Dennis. So people knew him as Dennis instead of Burglar Badman. He was a very lonely man.

Discussing this story

As Joe had emerged from his preoccupation with the reality of
the id, the stories became brief and to the point, having the
consistent shape of a problem and its solution. We sympathized
with Danny for his feelings are familiar. His efforts to deal with
these (the phobic reaction, the grief in bereavement and manic
defence) are all within the area of shared reality.

Through creativity Joe had survived the traumatic failure of
life's continuity as a family triad. From his dilemma of the
instinct to both create and destroy, Joe was saved by a manic
defence that would make his heartbreak seem funny until he
was old enough to deal with it. This resolve seemed successful
during latency; but as Joe approached puberty he needed to
evoke Burglar Badman again – the eighth story – to protect
him from the culture of adolescent delinquency and to express
and realize a depressed mood.

This time he wrote the story for himself and the maturity of
his handwriting indicated the positive change. This story had
many other indications of maturity, such as the use of decision-
making – 'One day the burglar decided to do a mugging...'.
This indicates psychic distancing from his destructive impulse
in light of the superego and established moral values. The
Badman decides that mugging is not fair and burglary is not a
good option as it results in a prison sentence. Turning for help
from his delinquent friends he finds them executed for crime.
He buys alcohol and a fake identity but in this disguise the
Burglar as a result is a very lonely man.

Joe's story stirs our compassion: it symbolizes the condi-
tion that is familiar to us all.

This interaction of the two basic instincts with and
against each other give rise to the whole variegation of

the phenomena of life... This is one of the dangers to health to which mankind become subject on their path to cultural development. (Freud 1949a, pp.6–7)

6

Discussion of Joe's Stories

> We are obliged to regard it [dream material] as part of
> the archaic heritage which a child brings with him into
> the world...as a result of the experiences of his
> ancestors. ... The governing laws of logic have no sway
> in the unconscious... (Freud 1949a, pp.28–31)

These stories are an extraordinary example of *archaic heritage*
for, when we interpret them, we discover the ancient tragedy of
Oedipus unfolding in the unconscious fantasy of a seven-
year-old boy when, like Oedipus the king, his assumption of
life's continuity had been destroyed. The symbolism in Joe's
stories appears to confirm Freud's theory of the psychosexual
developmental instincts displayed during his therapeutic regression, and then a return to the phallic stage of development.
This revelation impressed me to the extent that I was forced to
search for the words that would bridge the distance between
poetic and conceptual thought.

I find Freud's hypothesis amply explains the shock Joe
suffered: that our mental functions are based on creative and
destructive instincts fused in mental health. It must be admitted
that many children survive the trauma of a broken home
without obvious mental breakdown, so I suppose that he was a
particularly sensitive and vulnerable seven-year-old who depended on the unfailing support that his mother gave him.

However, Joe was at first overwhelmed by the enormity of his feelings about the broken home until I appeared to be a neutral transference object and he could discover a mythic image of destruction in the Burglar Badman. He had reacted to his anxiety by repressing all emotion and instead exhibited and was exhausted by serious hyperactivity.

Freud believed that, as creativity helps us to mentally bind issues together, a destructive attitude can separate and dissolve bonds. Therefore Joe was able through active story making to 'gather up' the concept of a good father and combine this with the presence of the bad father. Destructive and ambivalent feelings towards his father fill the first four stories but in the second four he can reclaim a more positive attitude.

At first the fantasy of patricide was symbolized by the id as a shitting dog whose anal sadism evoked the need for control by the superego (police) and whose oral conflict appears during the second story in stolen food that makes him ill. The Burglar takes the role of the undifferentiated ego/id, while non-functioning police act for the weakened superego. 'When the superego begins to be formed, considerable amounts of the aggressive instinct become fixated within the ego and operate there in a self-destructive fashion' (Freud 1949a, p.7).

The burglar is first seen as a Badman, then he becomes an anti-hero, a role that persists for several stories. The role later enlarges to encompass a relationship to Joe's female element. The theme of Joe's split home continues in ambivalence towards his parents: however, they come to be represented by the Badman and the lady, who complete their part in marriage.

Then the fourth story falls for a time into total regression, briefly exhibiting fantasies of oral incorporation before developing the theme of erotic love. The Badman and the lady leave the scene, Joe turns from this regressive phase, and in the fifth story they are replaced by Goodman. Goodman is now the ego-ideal, the purveyor of whole food; here a new character appears as a friend called Ryan, together with the stranger, who represents the destructive aspect of the superego. Between these fourth and fifth stories there seems to be a real abandoning of the id's influence and the ambivalence which was destroying his feelings.

Joe's stories continue by echoing the myth of Oedipus, for, as Goodman wanted to be a perfect friend, Oedipus wanted to be a perfect king. But both failed. The stranger (and the sphinx) cannot really be overthrown while heroes remain married to their mothers. The ego seems prepared to emancipate him – the girlfriend is now separate from the Oedipal mother.

The final part of the myth establishes Danny as a wee boy whose strengthened ego endures the inevitable mourning of the Oedipus complex and the depressive position which follows:

> She, the girlfriend of Danny, died one day and Danny was crying every day of his life and he just had to get on with his own life… Danny decided to do something about it so it would seem very funny because he would tell his mummy what happened about a year ago, when he was 20.

Danny's use of humour against the depressive position presents a typical picture of the psychic life of a seven-year-old.

A little later I was glad to hear that Joe had returned to his *own* everyday life.

He sent no more drawings or stories. However, some years later his mother discovered post-Oedipal Badman story (the eighth and last) which was needed by him at the time to explain his depression. Joe had not asked for his mother's help in writing this as he now could evoke the Badman for himself. His use of creative initiative suggests that it will continue to serve him during his future life.

7

Considerations of the Way in Which a Disturbed State was Resolved

> I am thinking of something that is in the common pool of humanity, into which individuals and groups of people may contribute, and from which we may all draw *if we have somewhere to put what we find.* (Winnicott 1982, p.99)

In this chapter I offer some general observations of Joe's art that can be seen regularly in our sessions with other children and adults who spontaneously use drawing, painting, clay or writing in their efforts to assimilate traumatic experiences.

Rycroft describes the psychoanalytic interpretation of trauma and our responses: 'any totally unexpected experience which the subject is unable to assimilate. The immediate response to psychological trauma is shock; the later effects are either spontaneous recovery...or the development of a traumatic neurosis' (Rycroft 1972, p.187). A physical response may also be immediate, for example a general loss of ability to think, or a partial amnesia. Joe's mother reported his symptoms as 'hyperactive and crazy behaviour'; they might seem to fit an interpretation of traumatic neurosis rather than the lack of insight referring to psychosis. She said that 'he knows about the divorce but he doesn't understand it'.

As I had no direct contact with Joe, I could not form any ideas about the pathological quality of his behaviour, but it was clear that avid attention to the drawings and stories had a great deal to do with his recovery. My interest here is with the *stages* in his recovery that are reflected in his art, for they indicate an innate process of self-healing that might be disturbed or even disrupted by untimely intervention, such as medication.

Joe's drawings show how the process of assimilating the trauma began in thoughtless gestures and came to form a house in the large scale of sensuous Archaic Linear art, normal for his age and stage (Simon 1992, 1997). But this stereotype drawing brought to consciousness his broken home and his anxiety about the divorce that seemed to threaten the very structure of his life. When such thoughtless gestures with a pen or pencil are seen to reflect a repressed fear, even momentarily revealed, some patients may violently repulse or destroy the image. However, others like Joe can deal with the traumatic memory and tolerate consciousness if they have a place or person – '*somewhere to put what we find*' (Winnicott 1982, p.99).

Joe's ego strength is reflected in the second drawing that symbolizes the divorce as two houses, each with half a roof. Here is a shift to the Traditional Linear style of conceptual art that may include words (Simon 1992, 1997), directing his anxiety towards assimilation through being able to 'think' symbolically or realistically; we discern a therapeutic sequence. Joe's aggression appears as a little figure, standing near the houses, with the *words* 'Burglar Badman' epitomizing anger towards his parents that was becoming conscious. By collaboration, Joe and his mother began to heal the split in his self-image when she wrote down his words, enabling him to verbalize his fear in various degrees of psychic projection. The symbolic figures included the Badman (Joe) having to act out his rage and incestuous wishes towards the lady.

These emotions showed the value and necessity for therapeutic regression during the process of the will to recover. In Joe's case it was first expressed in basic oral and anal terms through the created object, followed by the 'upward' thrust of reintegration where his creative urge to go forward and let go of incestuous desires enabled him to assimilate his regressed needs. Such fantasies and our nightmare defences against them are not untypical in dreams and usually fade with the passage of time but are revived in Joe and others who suffer traumatic shock.

How then did Joe recover? We can interpret the evidence of his stories as a symbolic compromise between the male and female elements in himself when he offered the girlfriend (in himself) the role of bisexual Burglaranna man before taking the great step towards the psychic integration that appreciates mutual love. To achieve this Joe had to sacrifice primary love to the Oedipus complex. Danny's girlfriend had to die. How was it possible for a small boy to form this extraordinarily condensed version of the Oedipal myth to its resolution in the depressive position? It is most unlikely that Joe had heard of the myth or could recreate it, unless Danny is seen as an example of creative instinct that includes the potential contained in Freud's hypothesis of an *archaic heritage*. Joe was successfully able to use the idea of a 'Mrs Simon' as a transference object and his panic became manageable when he could communicate to her – and, through her, to himself.

The art therapist's role, I believe, is to promote self-healing through the patient's own initiative. Joe's therapy is a unique example of non-intervention because it is a record of a process that occurs when time and place are right. One might say that the therapist is needed to see that nothing interrupts this process. I am reminded of Winnicott's plea: 'If only we can wait the patient arrives at understanding creatively and with immense joy, and I now enjoy this joy more than I used to enjoy the sense of having been clever' (Winnicott 1982, p.86).

Winnicott's term 'environmental provision' (Winnicott 1982, p.66) seems an appropriate description of Joe's mother's willing attention and her trust in the healing power of creativity. She provided a sketchbook and felt-tip pen and then wrote the stories to his dictation. The first drawing unconsciously expressed the reality of his broken home and by turning the paper over he demonstrated the necessity for a 'clean sheet', acknowledging two homes with the infantile Badman beside them. When Joe surrendered the Badman in the fifth story, we see how the ego-ideal transformed the subjective object towards the 'object objectively perceived':

> When I speak of the use of an object, however, I take object-relating for granted, and add new features that involve the nature and the behaviour of the object. For instance, the object, if it is to be used, must necessarily be real in the sense of being part of shared reality, not a bundle of projections. It is this, I think, that makes for the world of difference that there is between relating and usage. (Winnicott 1982, p.88)

Can there be a spontaneous recovery from mental illness? This appears to be possible when innate creativity allows both sensuous and emotional states to become conscious and be worked through in safety. I believe that creative art is always symbolic; below an apparent subject there is latent, universal meaning that is consciously or unconsciously recognized by its creator.

Joe's drawings and stories presented his feelings, exposing their meaning for him in the way that he could tolerate.

8

Summary

> It is creative apperception more than anything else that makes the individual feel that life is worth living. (Winnicott 1982, p.65)

This book is concerned with the creative apperception of a small boy who was able to escape mental illness by producing 'something out of himself' (Balint 1986, p.24) – two drawings and eight stories. Creativity is an instinct common to all, as a method of self-preservation; extending from this is the capacity to 'play'. Play can be seen as a random search for some integrating forms that satisfy the inner and outer realities of both sensuous and emotional life, as well as giving them aesthetic shape.

Freud distinguishes normal life as fusion between the creative and destructive instincts appearing to be correlated in a work of art, holding both together: this does not preclude the later use of recollection which is essential for creative thought. Joe was able to recover through making conscious his conflicts in the form of the Badman. These stories could have been seen by Freud and also Jung (1967, p.185) as examples of the 'archaic heritage' (or archetypes) that we all possess in our unconscious. In particular conditions of stress these are capable of becoming conscious in the form of familiar myths and fairy tales.

The first stories revealed Joe's need to regress deeply and the self-healing process which followed allowed the myth of Oedipus to emerge together with its inevitable conclusion in the depressive position. This enabled him to relinquish primary love. His myth followed this archaic pattern which we recognize in the structure of a work of art.

Fantasies which are essentially visual can be verbalized if there is someone to receive them. This seven-year-old boy used his 'mother's friend' (myself) as a reliable transference object for the drawings and stories to develop: his mother's *actual* patience and attention gave him the necessary time to achieve this. Joe gives us a direct example of the positive value of such non-interpreted art and it remains for us to properly understand it. The *style* of communication, whether pictorial or verbal, indicates the attitude and mood of its creator. Consciously or unconsciously, we respond to the way a communication is presented and the success of the therapy depends upon the quality of response.

Joe's symbolism anticipated the healing power of poetic myth that we laboriously rediscover through the language of psychoanalysis.

References

Balint, M. (1986) *The Basic Fault*. London: Tavistock Publications.

Freud, S. (1948) *An Autobiographical Study*. London: Hogarth Press.

Freud, S. (1949a) *An Outline of Psychoanalysis*. London: Hogarth Press.

Freud, S. (1949b) *The Ego and the Id*. London: Hogarth Press.

Jung, C.G. (1967) *Memories, Dreams, Reflections*. London: Collins, Fontana.

Kellogg, R. (1970) *Analysing Children's Art*. Palo Alta, California: Mayfield Publishing Company.

Klein, M. (1940) 'Mourning and its relation to manic-depressive states.' In *Contributions to Psychoanalysis 1921–1945*. London: Hogarth Press and the Institute of Psycho-Analysis 1948.

Kris, E. (1973) *Psychoanalytic Explorations in Art*. New York: Schocken Books.

Milner, M. (1987) *The Suppressed Madness of Sane Men*. London: Tavistock.

Rycroft, C. (1972) *A Critical Dictionary of Psychoanalysis*. London: Penguin.

Simon, R.M. (1992) *The Symbolism of Style*. London: Routledge.

Simon, R.M. (1997) *Symbolic Images in Art as Therapy*. London: Routledge.

Winnicott, D.W. (1982) *Playing and Reality*. London: Tavistock.

Index